ESTATE PUBLICATIONS

MEDWAY
GILLINGHAM

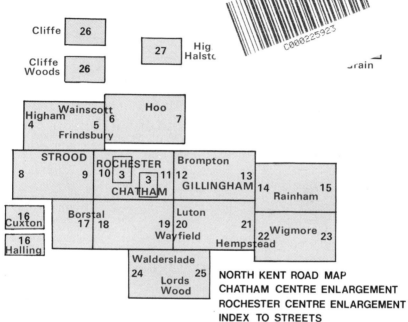

Cliffe | 26

Cliffe Woods | 26

27 | Hig Halstc

⌐rain

Higham 4 | Wainscott 5 | Hoo 7

Frindsbury

STROOD 8 9 | ROCHESTER 10 3 | 3 11 | Brompton 12 13

CHATHAM | GILLINGHAM 14 | 15

Rainham

16 Cuxton

16 Halling

Borstal 17 18 | 19 20 Luton | 21

Wayfield

22 Wigmore 23

Hempstead

Walderslade 24 | 25 Lords Wood

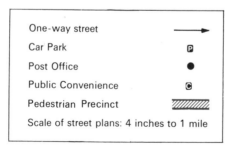

One-way street	→
Car Park	P
Post Office	●
Public Convenience	C
Pedestrian Precinct	▨

Scale of street plans: 4 inches to 1 mile

Street plans prepared and published by ESTATE PUBLICATIONS, Bridewell House, Tenterden, Kent and based upon the ORDNANCE SURVEY maps with the sanction of the controller of H.M. Stationery Office.

The publishers acknowledge the co-operation of Medway borough council and Gillingham borough council in the preparation of these maps.

0 86084 237 1

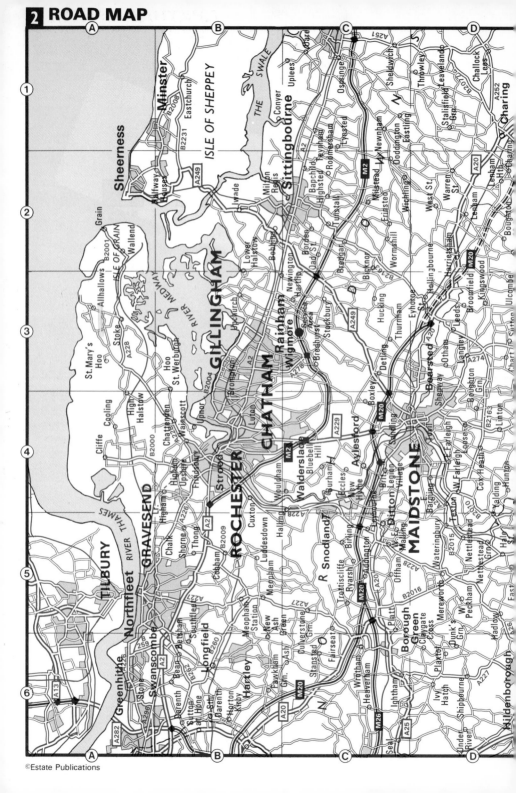

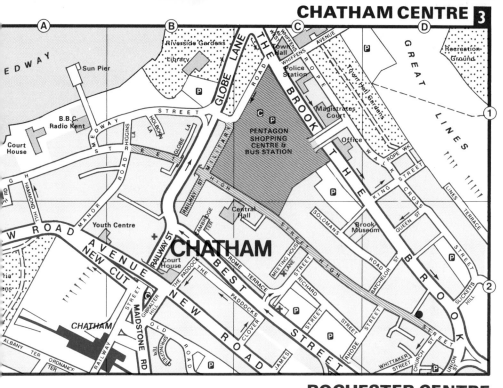

ROCHESTER CENTRE

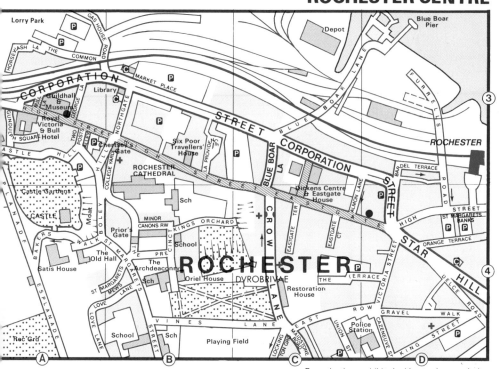

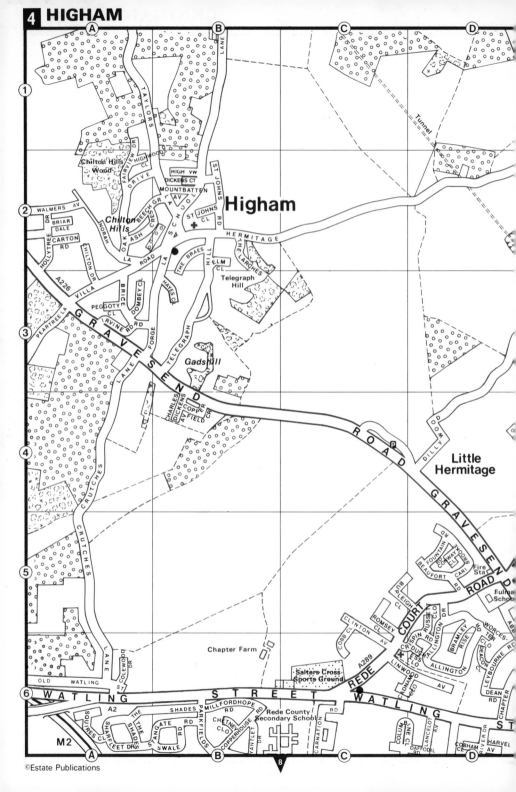

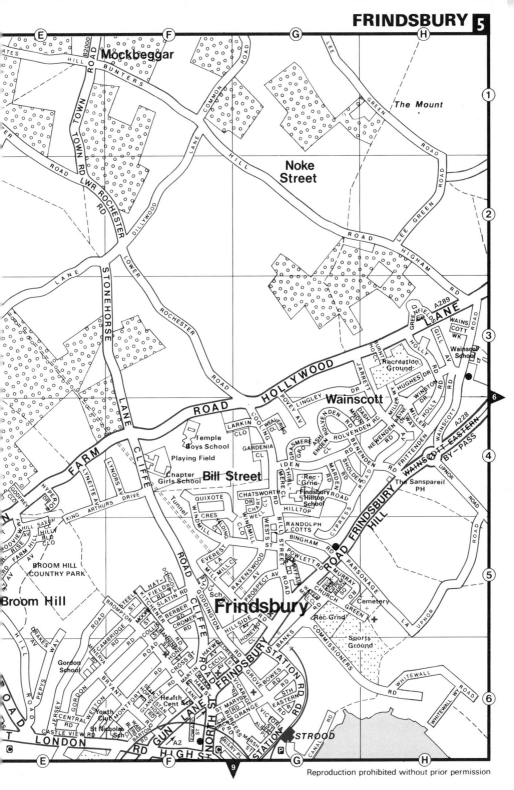

Ash Plantation

Ash Wood

Round Top Wood

Chattenden Farm

Deangate Ridge Municipal Go

Wind Pl

NORTH TER

CENTRAL TER

Playing Field

ELM-WOOD RD

SWINTON RD

LODGE HILL LA

Playing Field

CHATTENDEN BARRACKS

KIRBY

CHILLIWACK RD

Rams Bottom Wood

SIMMONDS

LINTORN

RATCLIFFE

Broad Stre

HAIG VILLAS

MAIN RO

KITCHENER

Chattenden

Sch

OLD SCH

HOO COMMON

BROADWOO

Playing Field

ELM AV

WOODFIELD

WAY

UPCHAT ROAD

FOUR ELMS HILL

BEACON HILL LANE

BALLS COTTS

Beacon Hill

HOO RD ROAD

A289

A228

WAINSCOTT EASTERN BY PASS

School

Arethuse Venture Centre

Medway Yacht Club

Cockhar

RIVER

Lower Upnor

Hall

UPNOR

Pier

Upnor Reach

Chatham Maritime Development

St. Mary's Js

School of Military Engineering

Upnor Castle

HIGH ST

ADMIRALTY RD

ADMIR

RICHMOND CL

CASTLE ST

TOWER HILL

Upper Upnor

BASIN 1

BASIN 2

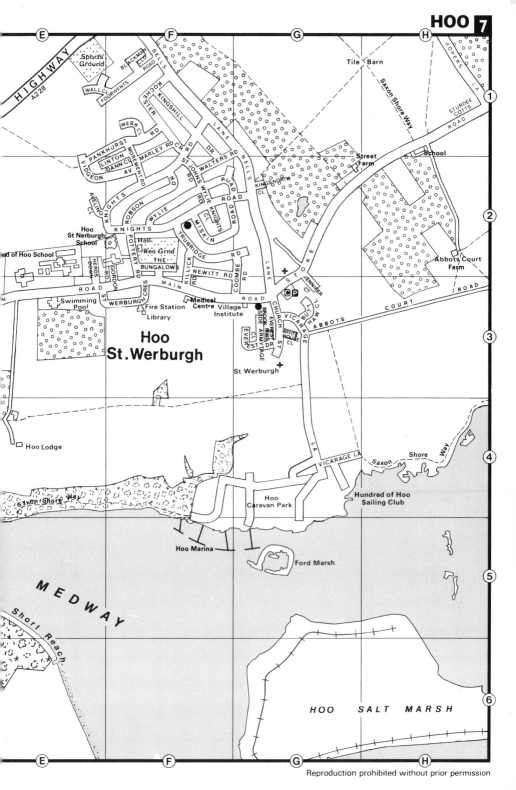

E F G H

1

Sports Ground
HIGHWAY A228
WALLC
FOURWENTS
BLACKMAN CLO
BELLS ROAD
ROCHESTER
KINGSHILL RD
WEBB CL
ROCHESTER RD
PANKHURST
LINTON
DANN CL
MOREMENT RD
VIDGEON
AV
MARLEY RD CR
ST JONS RD
WYLIE RD
WALTERS RD
KNIGHTS RD
LANE
BELLS
ROAD
KINGSNORTH
CL
Tile Barn

Saxon Shore Way

Street Farm

School

Sturdee COTTS ROAD
ROPERS LA

2

AVELING CL
KNIGHTS
ROBSON
WYLIE
KNIGHTS
DR
LANE
KNIGHTS
MISKIN
TRUBRIDGE

Hoo St Nerburgh School

ol of Hoo School

HERDS DOWN
GORDON
POTTERY RD
WERBURGH CRES
Hall
Red Grnd
THE BUNGALOWS
KILLICK RD
MAIN
NEWITT RD
COOMBE RD
ROAD

ROAD

Abbots Court Farm

3

Swimming Pool

Fire Station
Library
Medical Centre
Village Institute

Hoo
St.Werburgh

MAIN ROAD
CHURCH ST
BRSIDE
EVERESTS DR
CL
ARMYTAGE
EVEREST

CP

JENNIFER CT
ST
LA
BUHAW
VICARAGE
WHITE HOUSE CL

ABBOTS
COURT
ROAD

St Werburgh

4

Hoo Lodge

VICARAGE LA
Saxon Shore Way

Saxon Shore Way

Hoo Caravan Park

Hundred of Hoo Sailing Club

5

Hoo Marina

Ford Marsh

MEDWAY
Short Reach

6

HOO SALT MARSH

E F G H

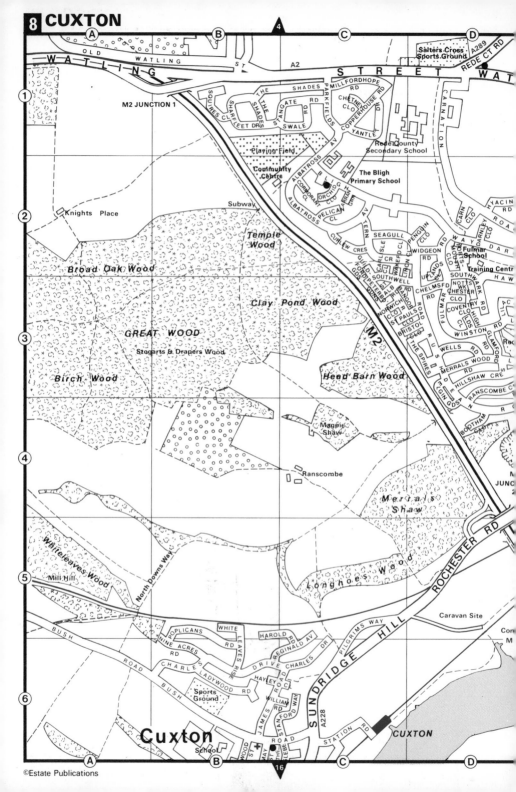

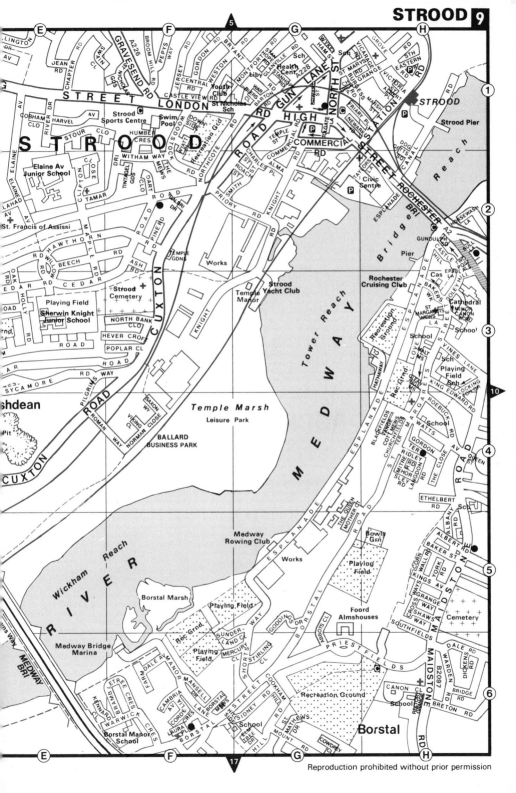

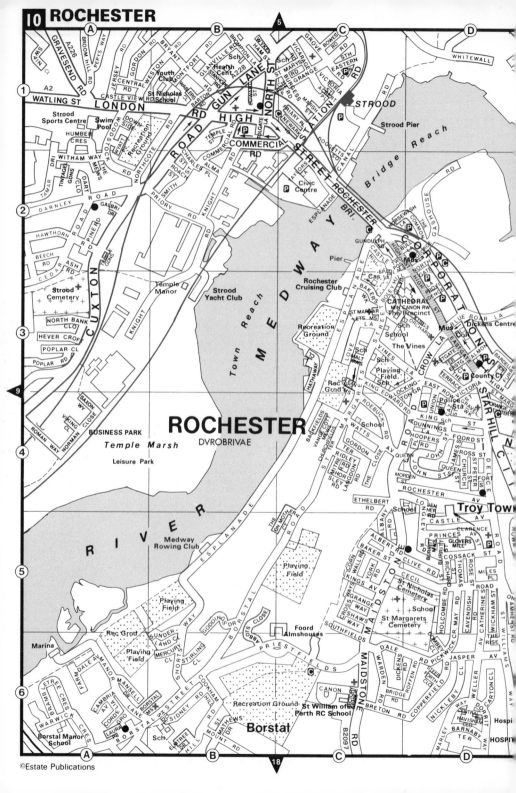

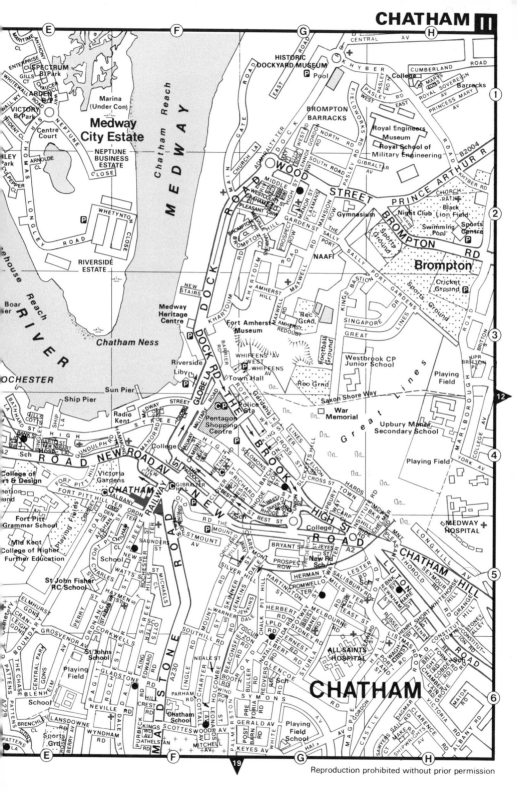

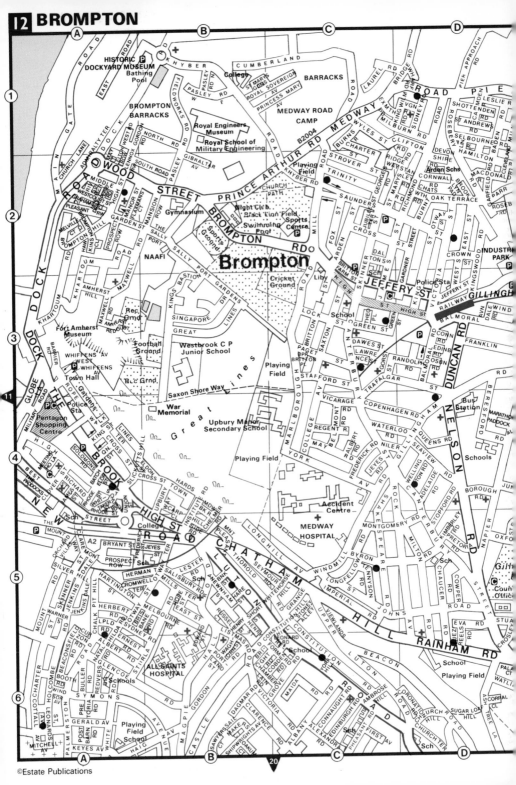

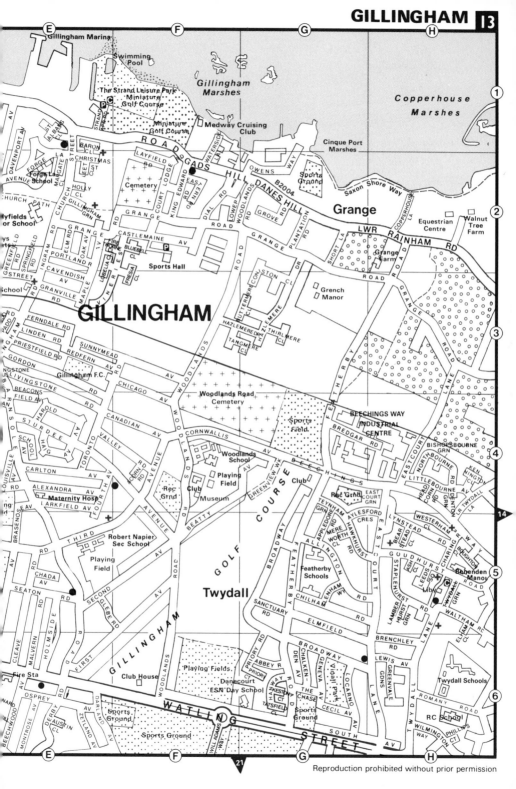

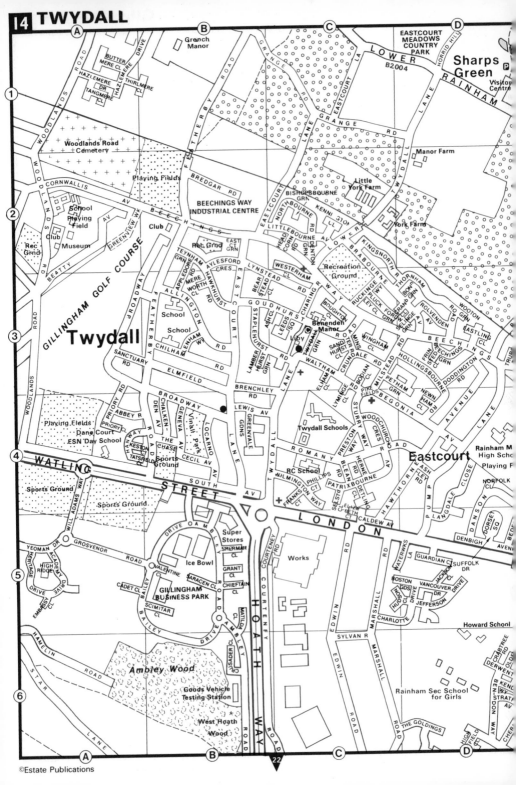

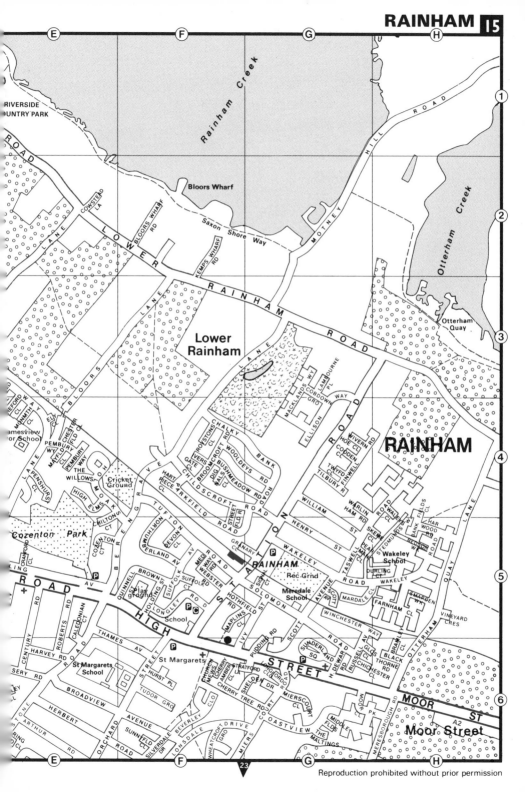

RIVERSIDE
COUNTRY PARK

Rainham Creek

Bloors Wharf

Saxon Shore Way

Otterham Creek

Otterham Quay

ROAD

LOWER

RAINHAM ROAD

Lower
Rainham

RAINHAM

Cozenton Park

Cricket Ground

HIGH STREET

RAINHAM

Rec Grnd

Wakeley School

Meredale School

St Margarets School

MOOR STREET

Moor Street

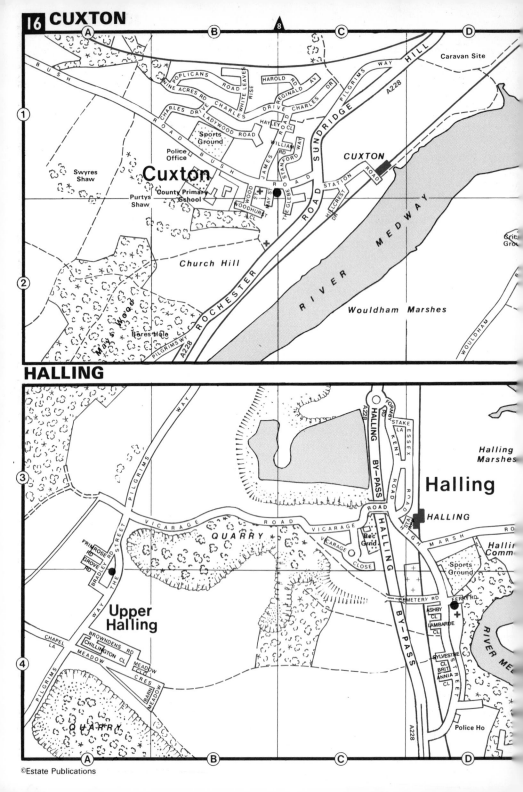

HALLING

©Estate Publications

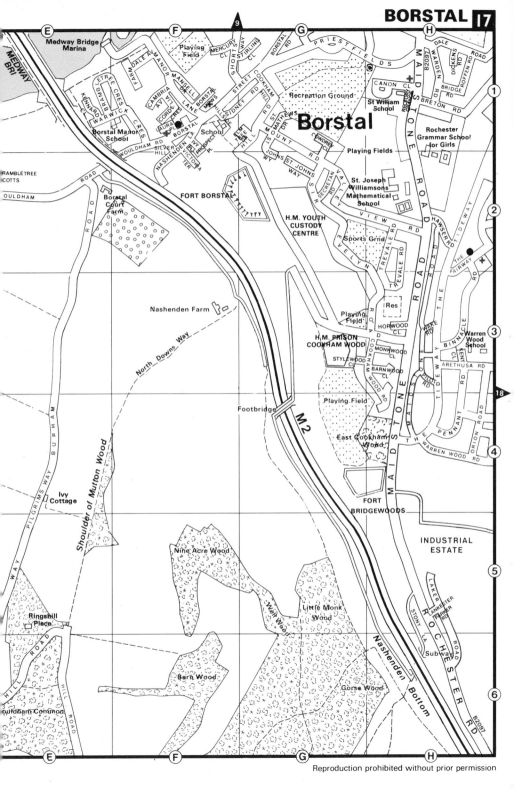

Borstal

Medway Bridge Marina

Playing Field

MEDWAY BRI

Recreation Ground

St William School

Rochester Grammar School for Girls

Borstal Manor School

School

Playing Fields

FORT BORSTAL

St. Joseph Williamsons Mathematical School

Borstal Court Farm

H.M. YOUTH CUSTODY CENTRE

Sports Grnd

RAMBLETREE COTTS

OULDHAM

Nashenden Farm

Playing Field

Res

H.M. PRISON COOKHAM WOOD

Warren Wood School

ARETHUSA RD

North Downs Way

Footbridge

Playing Field

East Cookham Wood

Ivy Cottage

FORT BRIDGEWOODS

INDUSTRIAL ESTATE

Ringshill Place

Nine Acre Wood

Little Monk Wood

Barn Wood

Gorse Wood

Subway

Ouldham Common

Nashenden Bottom

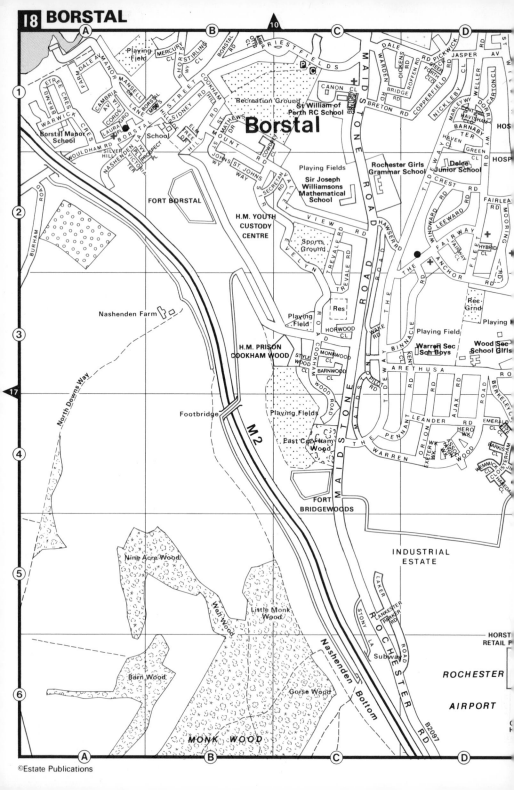

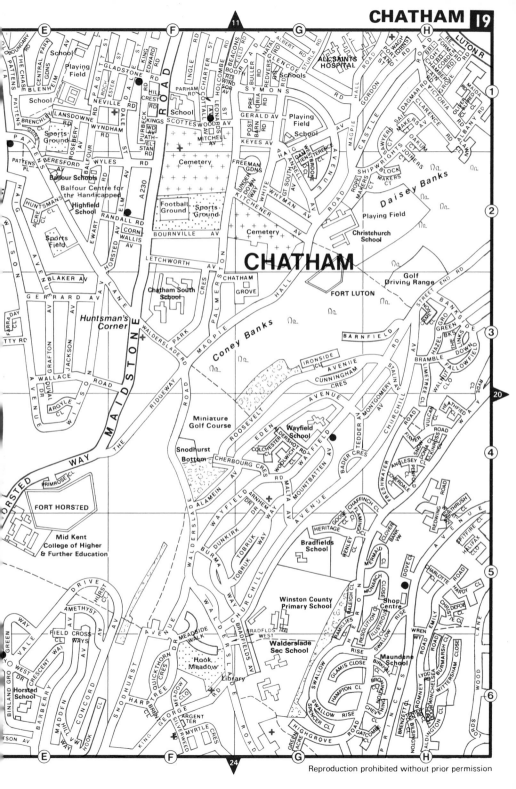

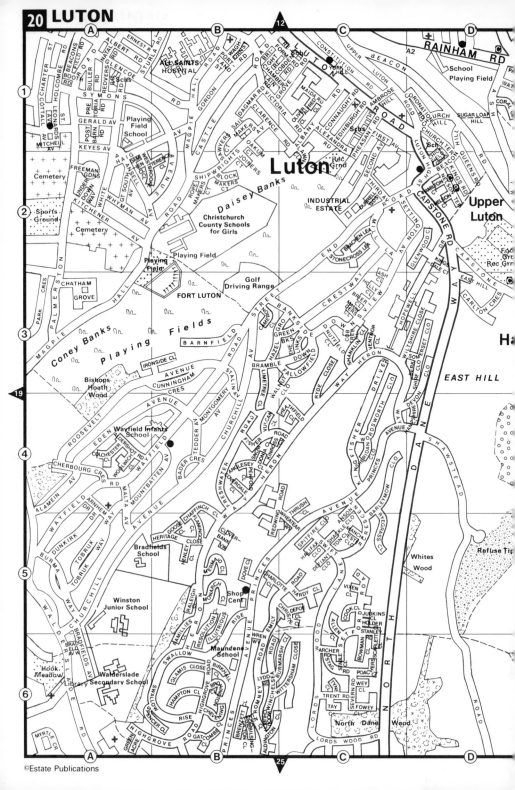

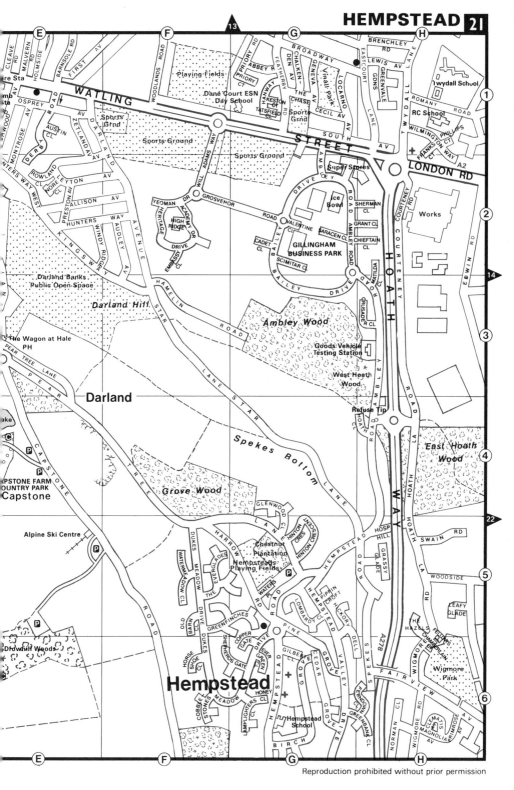

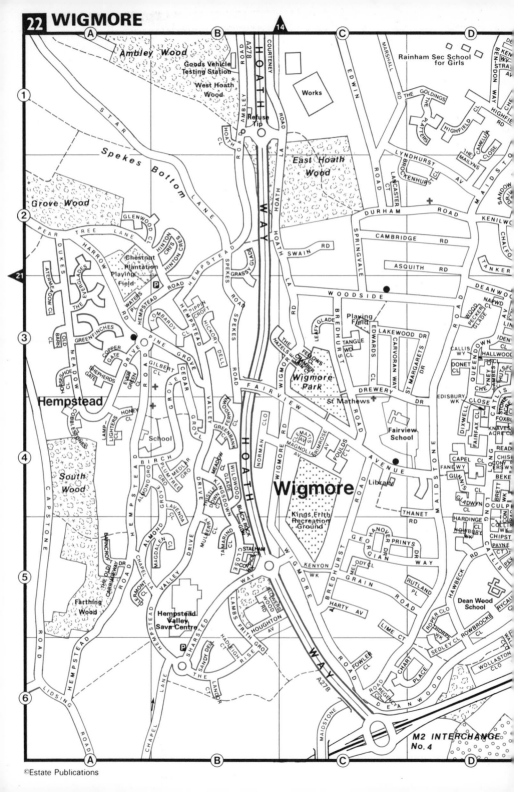

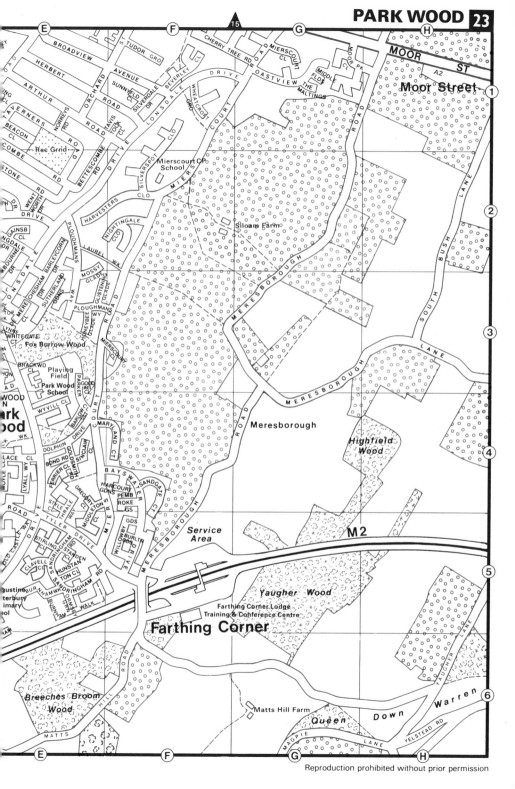

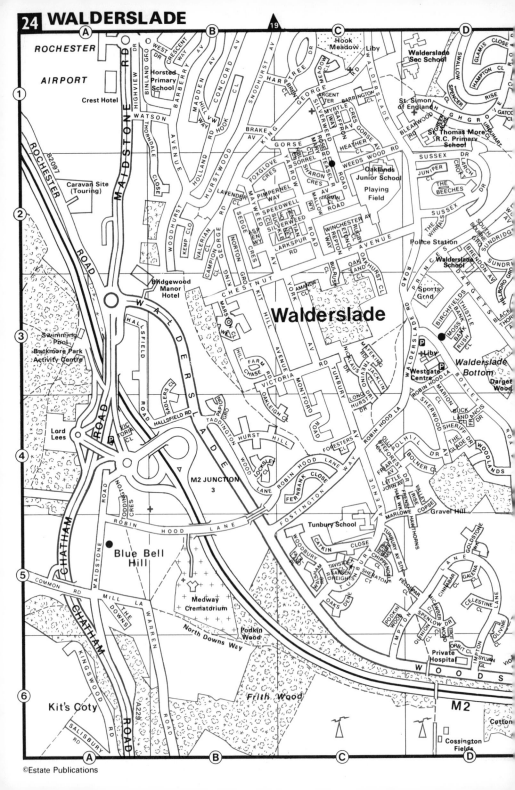

ROCHESTER

AIRPORT

19

Hook Meadow

Liby

Walderslade Sec School

Crest Hotel

Horsted Primary School

St. Simon of England

St. Thomas More R.C. Primary School

THE BEECHES

Caravan Site (Touring)

Bridgewood Manor Hotel

Oaklands Junior School

Playing Field

Police Station

Walderslade

Swimming Pool Buckmore Park Activity Centre

Walderslade School

Sports Grnd

Birchfields

Liby

Walderslade Bottom

Darget Wood

Westgate Centre

Lord Lees

M2 JUNCTION 3

Tunbury School

Gravel Hill

WOODLANDS

Blue Bell Hill

Medway Crematorium

North Downs Way

Podkin Wood

Private Hospital

WOODS

Kit's Coty

Frith Wood

M2

Cossington Fields

Cotton

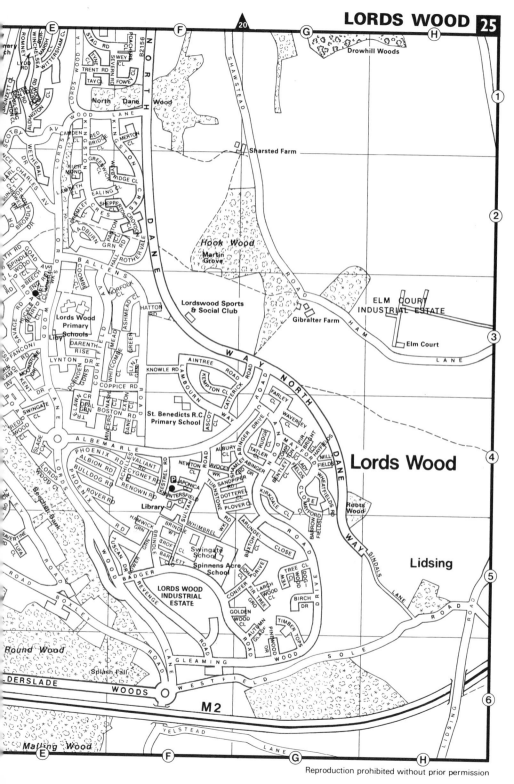

Drowhill Woods

Sharsted Farm

North Dane Wood

Hook Wood

Martin Grove

Lordswood Sports & Social Club

Gibralter Farm

ELM COURT INDUSTRIAL ESTATE

Elm Court

Lords Wood Primary Schools

St. Benedicts R.C Primary School

Lords Wood

Roots Wood

Library

Lidsing

Swingate School

Spinnens Acre School

LORDS WOOD INDUSTRIAL ESTATE

Round Wood

Splash Fall

DERSLADE WOODS

M 2

Malling Wood

YELSTEAD LANE

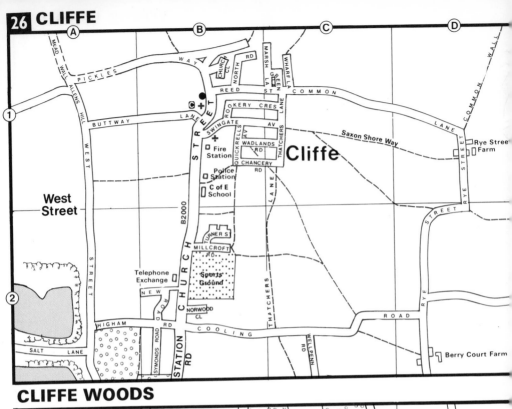

CLIFFE WOODS

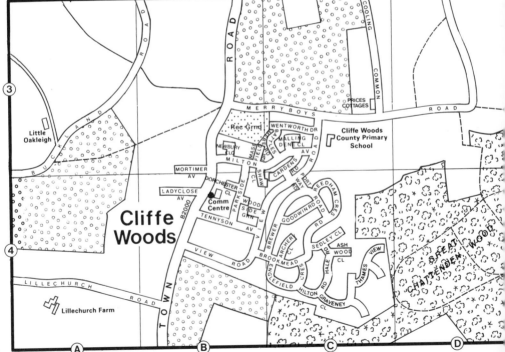

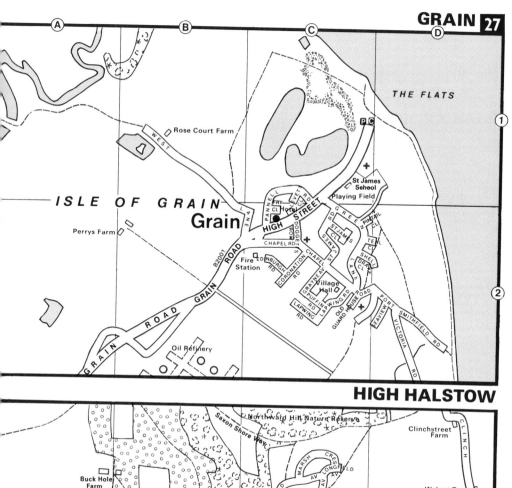

THE FLATS

(1)

Rose Court Farm

WEST

ISLE OF GRAIN

Grain

P C

St James
School
Playing Field

PANNELL CL

FERRY
CL

HIGH STREET

LEVEN RD

BROGGETS

GREEN RD

PINTAIL CL

Perrys Farm

CHAPEL RD

ST JAMES

ST JAMES CL

TEAL CL

SHELL DRA CL

B2001

ROAD

Fire
Station

EDINBURGH RD

CORONATION RD

CHAPEL RD

Village
Hall

BAYNEAV

PUFFIN AV

LAPWING RD

OLD HOUSE ROAD

GUARD HOUSE RD

PORT VICTORIA RD

BEAVER RD

SMITHFIELD RD

(2)

GRAIN

ROAD

Oil Refinery

HIGH HALSTOW

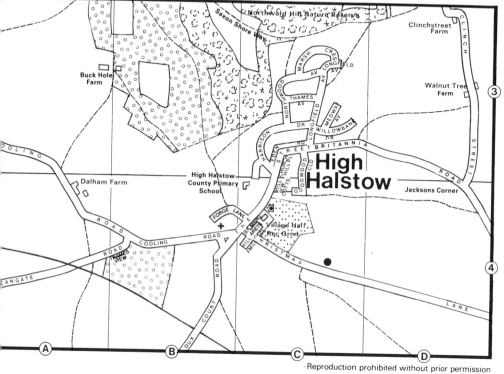

Northward Hill Nature Reserve

Saxon Shore Way

Clinchstreet
Farm

CLINCH

Buck Hole
Farm

MARSH CRES

LONGFIELD AV

LONGFIELD AV

Walnut Tree
Farm

(3)

THAMES
AV

NORTHDOWN DR

LONGFIELD DR

MEDWAY AV

WILLOWBANK DR

STREET ROAD

Dalham Farm

HARRISON DR

EDEN RD

STS HILLS RD

BRITANNIA

High
Halstow

COOLING

High Halstow
County Primary
School

High Halstow
County Primary
School

GODWOOD RD

Jacksons Corner

STREET ROAD

FORGE LANE

Village Hall
Rec Grnd

ROAD

COOLING

ROAD

ROAD

THAMES
VIEW

CHRISTMAS

LANE

(4)

NGATE

DUX COURT ROAD

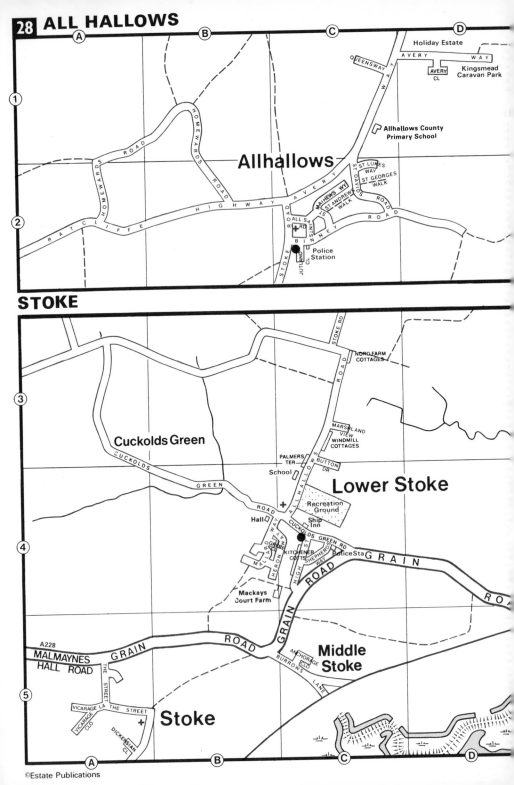

Allhallows

Holiday Estate

AVERY WAY

QUEENSWAY

AVERY CL

Kingsmead Caravan Park

Allhallows County Primary School

HOMEWARDS ROAD

HOMEWARDS ROAD

ROAD

HOMEWARDS

RATCLIFFE

HIGHWAY

AVERY

ST LUKES WAY
ST GEORGES WALK

ST DAVIDS

MALTHEWS WY
ST ANDREWS WALK

ROAD

ROAD

ALL SAINTS RD

STOKE ROAD

JUTLAND BINNEY

Police Station

STOKE

STOKE RD

ROAD

NORD FARM COTTAGES

Cuckolds Green

CUCKOLDS

GREEN

MARSH LAND VIEW WINDMILL COTTAGES

PALMERS TER

School

BUTTON DR

ALL HALLOWS

Lower Stoke

ROAD

Recreation Ground

Hall

Ship Inn

CUCKOLDS GREEN RD

KITCHENER COTTS

OGBRE WAY

HERON WAY

HIGH ST

SHEPHERD WAY

Police Sta

GRAIN ROAD

ROAD

Mackays Court Farm

GRAIN

ROAD

A228

MALMAYNES HALL ROAD

GRAIN ROAD

ANCHORAGE CLO

BURROWS LANE

Middle Stoke

THE STREET

VICARAGE LA

VICARAGE CLO

THE STREET

DICKENSIAN CL

Stoke

INDEX TO STREETS

...dex includes some
s for which there is
icient space on the
These names are
ded by an * and are
ved by the nearest
ing thoroughfare.

...DWAY

y Rd, Gillingham	13 G6
y Rd, Strood	4 D5
's Clo	9 G6
s Court Rd	7 G2
er Dri	25 G4
emy Dri	21 F2
es Rd	25 F4
n Rd	13 F4
Clo	19 E2
ide Rd	12 D4
rals Walk	25 E3
ralty Rd	6 B6
ralty Ter,	
mpton	11 G2
ralty Ter, Upnor	6 B6
an Rd	11 E5
ee Rd	25 F3
Rd	18 D4
ein Av	19 F4
ay Rd, Chatham	11 H6
ay Rd, Gillingham	13 E4
ay Rd, Rochester	9 H5
ay Ter, Brompton	12 D4
ay Ter, Chatham	3 A2
ross Av	8 C2
narle Rd	25 E4
t Pl	5 G6
t Rd, Chatham	11 G6
t Rd, Gillingham	12 C4
t Rd, Rochester	9 H5
n Pl	6 C5
n Rd	25 E4
y Clo	25 F4
shot Rd	20 A4
gton Clo	19 H6
ndra Av	13 E4
ndra Rd	20 C1
d Clo	20 C1
ints Rd	28 C2
Clo	20 C5
s Hill	26 A1
llows Rd	28 C4
gton Clo	4 D6
gton Rd	13 G5
n Av	21 E2
Pl	9 G2
n La	3 C4
nd Gro	22 A4
nda Clo	24 C3
ey Rd	22 B1
rose Hill	20 C1
hyst Av	19 E5
erst Hill	12 A3
erst Rd	10 D5
erst Redoubt	11 G3
or Rd	18 D2
orage Clo	28 C5
esey Clo	20 B4
l Av	19 G2
n Clo	20 C4
nys Way	5 H4
eby Clo	18 D4
edore Rd	13 G5
er Rd	20 C6
ery Clo	26 C4
n St	12 C2
usa Rd	17 D3
t Ter	24 C1
e Clo	19 E4
tage Clo	7 G3
em Dri	19 G4
de Clo	11 E2
Grn	8 C2
r Rd, Rainham	15 E6
r Rd, Rochester	10 D5
del Clo	25 G5
t Clo	25 F4
Clo, Luton	20 C2
Clo, Twydall	14 B3
res	4 A2
Rd	9 F2
ree La	20 D1
y Clo	16 D4
nden Clo	5 G4
ey Rd	14 D4
ead Clo	25 F3

Ashwood Clo	26 C4
Aspen Way	24 B2
Asquith Rd	22 D2
Association Walk	18 D4
Aston Clo	24 D4
Athelstan Rd	11 F6
Audley Av	21 F2
Austin Clo	21 E1
Autumn Glade	25 G5
Aveling Clo	7 E2
Avery Clo	28 D1
Avery Way	28 C2
Avocet Walk	25 F4
Avondale Rd	12 D3
Aylesford Cres	13 G4
Baden Rd	12 D1
Bader Cres	19 G4
Badger Rd	25 F5
Bailey Dri	14 A5
Baker St	9 H5
Bakers Walk	3 A4
Balfour Rd	6 B6
Ballens Rd	25 E2
Balls Cotts	6 B3
Balmer Clo	23 E1
Balmoral Rd	12 D3
Bangor Rd	8 C3
Bank Fields Clo	15 H5
Bank St	11 H5
Banks Rd	5 G5
Bankside	19 H3
Banning St	5 H5
Barberry Av	19 E6
Bardell Ter	3 D3
*Barfleur Manor,	
Middle St	3 D3
Barkis Clo	18 D4
Barleycorn Dri	23 E2
Barleymow Clo	20 C4
Barlow Clo	23 E4
Barn Meadow	16 A4
Barnaby Ter	10 D6
Barncroft Dri	22 A5
Barnfield	19 H3
Barnsole Rd	13 E3
Barnwood Clo	17 D3
Baron Clo	13 E1
Barrier Rd	11 F3
Barrington Clo	24 D1
Barrowfields	25 G4
Bartlett Clo	25 F5
Barton Rd	9 G1
Basi Clo	5 G5
Batchelor St	3 D2
Bath Hard La	11 E4
Battlesmere Rd	26 C3
Bayswater Dri	23 F4
Beacon Clo	23 E1
Beacon Hill	20 D2
Beacon Hill La	6 B4
Beacon Rd	20 C1
Beaconsfield Av	13 E4
Beaconsfield Rd	11 F6
Bearstead Clo	13 H5
Beatty Av	13 F5
Beatty Rd	19 E3
Beaufort Rd	4 D5
Bedford Av	14 D5
Bedson Walk	15 H5
Bedwin Clo	18 D4
Beech Gro	4 A2
Beech Rd	9 E2
Beechen Bank Rd	24 D4
Beeching Rd	25 E3
Beechings Grn	14 D3
Beechings Way	13 D3
Beechmore Dri	24 D4
Beechwood Av	21 E1
Begonia Av	14 C4
Beke Rd	22 D4
Bells La	7 F1
Belmont Rd	12 C4
Bendon Way	14 D6
Benenden Rd	5 G4
Bentley Clo	25 G4
Berber Rd	5 F5
Berengrave La	15 E5
Beresford Av	19 E2
Beresford Rd	18 D3
Berkeley Clo	20 D3
Berkshire Clo	19 E2
Best St	3 B2
Bettescombe Rd	15 F6
Beverley Clo	15 F6
Bill Street Rd	5 G5
Bingham Rd	5 G5

Bingley Rd	11 E4
Binland Gro	19 E6
Binnacle Rd	17 D3
Binney Rd	28 C2
Birch Dri	25 G5
Birch Gro	21 G6
Birchfields	24 D3
Birkhall Clo	20 B6
Birling Av	15 E5
Bishopsbourne Grn	13 H4
Black Rock Gdn	22 B4
Blackfields	9 H4
Blackman Clo	7 F1
Blackthorn Av	24 D3
Blackthorne Rd	15 H6
Blaker Av	19 E3
Bleakwood Rd	24 D1
Blean Rd	14 C4
Blenheim Av	11 E6
Bligh Way	8 C2
Blockmakers Ct	19 H2
Bloors La	15 E5
Bloors Wharf Rd	15 F2
Blowers Wood Clo	22 B5
Blue Boar La	3 C3
Bluebell Clo	13 F2
Bodian Clo	14 C3
Boley Hill	3 A4
Bolner Clo	24 D4
Bond Road	23 E4
Bonnington Grn	14 D3
Booth Rd	11 F6
Bootham Clo	8 D4
Borough Rd	12 D4
Borstal Mews	18 A1
Borstal Rd	9 G5
Borstal St	9 F6
Boston Gdns	14 C5
Boston Rd	25 E4
Boughton Clo	14 C3
Boundary Rd	3 A2
Bournville Av	19 F2
Bower Grn	25 F5
Bowes Rd	5 G6
Bowman Clo	20 C6
Boxley Rd	24 D3
Brabourne Av	14 C2
Bracken Lea	20 C2
Brackwood Clo	23 E3
Bradfields Av	19 G5
Bradfields Av West	19 G5
Bradley Rd	16 A4
Brake Av	24 B1
Bramble Down	19 H3
Brambletree Cottages	17 A2
Brambletree Cres	9 F6
Bramley Clo	15 H6
Bramley Rise	4 D5
Bransgore Av	22 D2
Brasenose Av	13 E5
Bredgar Rd	13 G4
Bredhurst Rd	22 C3
Brenchley Clo	19 E1
Brenchley Rd	13 H6
Brendon Av	24 D2
Brent Clo	19 F6
Brenzett Clo	20 B6
Breton Rd	10 C6
Brett Walk	22 D4
Brewer Rd	26 B4
Briar Dale	4 A2
Brice Rd	4 A3
Bridge Rd, Gillingham	12 D1
Bridge Rd, Medway	10 C6
Brier Clo	20 C3
Bright Rd	11 H6
Brindle Way	25 F5
Brisbane Rd	11 G5
Brissenden Clo	6 C5
Bristol Clo	8 D3
Britannia Clo	16 D4
Britannia Rd	27 C3
Britton Farm St	12 C2
Britton St	12 C3
Broadlands Dri	25 E2
Broadview Av	15 E6
Broadway	13 G5
Broadwood Rd	6 C3
Brockenhurst Clo	22 C2
Bromley Clo	25 E2
Brompton Clo	11 F2
Brompton Farm Rd	4 D5
Brompton Hill	11 F2
Brompton La	5 F5
Brompton Rd	11 H2
Bronington Clo	20 B6
Brook Side	7 G3

Brooklyn Paddock	12 D2
Brookmead Rd	26 B4
Broom Hill Rd	4 D5
Broomcroft Rd	15 F4
Brown Rd	15 F5
Browndens Rd	16 A4
Brownlow Copse	25 E4
Bryant Rd	5 F6
Bryant St	11 G5
Buckingham Rd	12 D3
Buckland Clo	24 D4
Buckland Rd	26 A3
Bull La	3 A3
Bulldog Rd	25 E4
Buller Rd	11 G6
Bulrush Clo	24 C2
Bumbles Clo	18 D4
Bunters Hill Rd	5 F1
Burgess Rd	5 G6
Burham Rd	17 A4
Burleigh Clo	4 C5
Burlington Gdns	23 F5
Burma Way	19 F5
Burmarsh Rd	20 B6
Burnham Walk	23 E5
Burns Rd	12 C1
Burnt House Clo	5 H3
Burnt Oak Ter	12 D2
Burrit Mews	10 D5
Burritt St	10 D5
Burrows La	28 C5
Bush Rd	16 A1
Bushmeadow Rd	15 F4
Butt Haw Clo	7 G3
Buttermere Clo	13 G3
Button Dri	28 C4
Buttway La	26 A1
Buxton Clo	25 G5
Byron Rd	12 C5
Cadet Clo	14 A5
Cadnam Clo	4 C6
Caldew Av	14 C5
Caledonian Ct	15 E5
Callans Clo	23 E3
Callis Way	24 D2
Cambria Av	9 F6
Cambridge Rd, Rainham	22 C2
Cambridge Rd, Strood	5 E6
Cambridge Ter	3 B2
Camden Clo	25 E1
Camden Rd	12 D1
Camellia Clo	22 D1
Cameron Clo	20 B3
Campion Clo	24 B2
Campleshon Rd	22 D3
Canadian Av	13 F4
Canal Rd	9 H2
Canon Clo	9 H6
Canterbury St	12 C3
Capel Clo	22 D4
Capstone Rd	20 D2
Cardens Rd	26 C3
Carisbrooke Rd	4 D5
Carlisle Clo	8 C2
Carlton Av	13 E4
Carlton Cres	20 D3
Carn Clo	8 D2
Carnation Rd	4 C6
Carpeaux Clo	11 G4
Carton Clo	10 D6
Carton Rd	4 A2
Carvoran Way	22 C3
Castle Av	10 D5
Castle Hill	3 A3
Castle Rd	11 H6
Castle St	6 B6
Castle View Rd	5 E6
Castlemaine Av	13 F2
Catherine St	10 D5
Catkin Clo	24 C5
Catterick Rd	25 F4
Cavendish Av	13 E2
Cavendish Rd	10 D5
Cazeneuve St	3 D4
Cecil Av, Frindsbury	5 F6
Cecil Av, Rainham	13 G6
Cecil Rd	10 D5
Cedar Gro	21 G6
Cedar Rd	9 E3
Celestine Clo	24 D5
Cemetery Rd	16 C4
Central Av	11 G1
Central Par	10 D6
Central Park Gdns	11 E6
Central Rd	5 E6
Central Ter	6 B1

Century Rd	15 E6
Chada Av	13 E5
Chaffinch Clo	20 B5
Chalfont Dri	22 D2
Chalk Pit Hill	11 G5
Chalkenden Av	13 G6
Chalky Bank Rd	15 F4
Chamberlain Ct	21 H6
Chamberlain Rd	11 H6
Chancery Rd	26 B1
Chapel La, Upr Halling	16 A5
Chapel La, Wigmore	22 C3
Chapel Rd	27 C1
Chapter Rd	4 D6
Charing Rd	13 H5
Charles Dickens Av	4 B4
Charles Dri	16 B1
Charles St, Chatham	11 E5
Charles St, Strood	9 G2
Charlotte Clo	20 B5
Charlotte Dri	14 C5
Chart Pl	22 C6
Charter St, Chatham	11 F6
Charter St, Gillingham	12 C1
Chartwell Clo	5 G4
Chatham Gro	19 F3
Chatham Hill	11 H5
Chatham Rd	24 A5
Chatsworth Dri	5 G4
Chatsworth Rd	12 D2
Chattenden La	6 B3
Chaucer Clo	11 E1
Chaucer Rd	12 D5
Chegwell Dri	25 E2
Chelmer Rd	11 H5
Chelmsford Rd	8 D3
Cherbourg Cres	19 G4
Cheriton Rd	14 D6
Cherry Amber Clo	15 F6
Cherry Tree Rd	15 F6
Chesham Dri	23 E3
Chester Clo	8 D3
Chester Rd	12 D6
Chesterfield Clo	15 E4
Chestnut Av	24 B3
Chestnut Rd	8 D3
Chetney Clo	4 B6
Chevening Clo	24 D1
Cheyney Clo	22 D3
Chicago Av	13 F3
Chichester Clo	15 G6
Chickfield Gdns	20 D2
Chieftain Clo	21 H2
Childscroft Rd	15 F4
Chilham Clo	11 F5
Chilham Rd	13 G5
Chillington Clo	16 A4
Chilliwack Rd	6 B2
Chilton Ct	15 E4
Chilton St	4 A2
Chippendale Clo	24 C5
Chipstead Rd	22 D5
Chislet Walk	22 D4
Christie Clo	20 C5
Christmas La	27 C4
Christmas St	13 E2
Church Clo	13 E2
Church Green	5 G5
Church Hill	20 D1
Church Hill Pl	27 C3
Church La	11 F2
Church Mews	15 F6
Church Path, Brompton	11 H2
Church Path, Gillingham	13 E2
Church Path, Strood	5 F6
Church St, Chatham	3 D2
Church St, Cliffe	26 B2
Church St, Gillingham	13 E2
Church St, Hoo	7 G3
Church St, Rochester	10 D4
Church Ter	20 D1
Churchfields Ter	9 H4
Churchill Av	19 G5
Chute Clo	22 D4
Cinnabar Clo	24 D5
City Way	11 F3
Clandon Rd	25 G4
Claremont Way	11 G5
Clarence Av	10 D5
Clarence Rd	11 H6
Clavell Clo	23 E5
Cleave Rd	13 E6
Clematis Av	22 C4
Clermont Clo	25 E1
Cleveland Rd	12 D2
Cliffe Rd	5 F4
Clifton Clo	9 E2

Street	Ref
Clifton Rd	12 D1
Clinch St	27 D3
Clinton Av	4 C5
Clive Rd	10 D5
Cloisterham Rd	18 D4
Clover St	3 C2
Cobb Clo	4 C5
Cobblestones	21 F6
Cobden Rd	11 H6
Cobdown Gro	15 G3
Cobham Clo	9 E1
Cobtree Clo	20 C3
Colchester Clo	20 A4
Colewood Dri	4 A6
College Av	12 C4
College Yard	3 B3
Collet Walk	23 E5
Colling Walk	22 D5
Collis St	5 F5
Columbine Clo	4 C6
Columbine Rd	8 D1
Commercial Rd	9 G1
Commissioners Rd	5 G5
Common La	26 C1
Common Rd, Mockbeggar	5 F1
Common Rd, Walderslade	24 A5
Common Wall	26 D1
Compton Clo	25 G4
Concord Av	19 E6
Conifer Dri	25 G5
Coniston Clo	13 G3
Connaught Rd, Gillingham	12 D3
Connaught Rd, Luton	20 C1
Conrad Clo	22 D4
Constitution Hill	11 H5
Constitution Rd	20 C1
Conway Clo	4 D5
Conyers Way	22 D4
Cooden Clo	15 G4
Cook Clo	20 C5
Cookham Hill	9 G6
Cookham Wood Rd	17 D3
Cooling Common	26 C3
Cooling Rd, Cliffe	26 B2
Cooling Rd, High Halstow	27 A3
Cooling Rd, Wainscott	5 G4
Coombe Clo	25 E2
Coombe Rd	7 G3
Cooper Rd	24 D3
Copenhagen Rd	12 C4
Copper Gate	21 G6
Copperfield Cres	4 B4
Copperfield Rd	10 D6
Copperhouse La	13 H2
Copperhouse Rd	4 B6
Coppertree Walk	25 F5
Coppice Rd	25 E3
Coppice Walk	22 B5
Cordelia Cres	9 F6
Corkwell St	11 E5
Cormorant Clo	8 C2
Cornwall Rd, Gillingham	12 D2
Cornwall Rd, Rochester	9 H5
Cornwallis Av, Chatham	19 F2
Cornwallis Av, Gillingham	13 F4
Coronation Rd, Grain	27 C2
Coronation Rd, Luton	20 D1
Corporation Rd	12 D2
Corporation St	3 A3
Corral Clo	12 D6
Cossack St	10 D5
Cossington Rd	25 E5
Cottall Av	11 F6
Coulman St	13 E4
Court Lodge Rd	13 F2
Courteney Rd	14 B5
Courtfield Av	25 E3
Coventry Clo	8 D3
Coverdale Clo	20 B4
Cowbeck Clo	22 D3
Cowdrey Clo	18 B1
Cowper Rd	12 D5
Cowstead La	15 E2
Cozenton Ct	15 E5
Crabtree Rd	14 D6
Cranbrook Clo	14 D3
Cranford Clo	15 E5
Cranleigh Gdns	11 E5
Crescent Way	19 E6
Cressey Ct	11 E4
Crest Rd	18 D2
Crestway	20 C3
Crispe Clo	22 D4
Crispin Rd	4 C5
Croft Clo	25 F5
Cromer Rd	5 F5
Cromwell Ter	11 G5
Crosley Rd	12 D6
Cross St, Chatham	3 D1
Cross St, Frindsbury	5 F6
Cross St, Gillingham	12 C2
Crossways, Rochester	9 H5
Crossways, Walderslade	19 E5
Crow La	3 C4
Crown St	12 D2
Croydon Clo	25 F2
Crundale Rd	14 C3
Crusader Clo	21 H3
Crutches La	4 A4
Cuckolds Green Rd	28 C4
Culpepper Clo	11 E2
Culpepper Rd	22 D4
Cumberland Rd	11 H1
Cunningham Cres	19 G3
Curlew Cres	8 C2
Curzon Rd	11 G5
Cuxton Rd	9 E4
Cygnet Rd	25 F4
Cypress Rd	5 G5
Daffodil Rd	9 E1
Dagmar Rd	11 H6
Dale Rd	10 C6
Dale St	11 F6
Dalton St	12 C2
Damien Clo	19 G2
Dane Clo	25 F4
Danes Hill	13 G2
Danson Way	14 D5
Darenth Rise	25 E3
Dargets Rd	24 D3
Darland Av	21 E1
Darnley Clo	8 D2
Darnley Rd	8 D2
Dart Clo	9 F2
Dashmonden Clo	5 H4
Davenport Av	13 E2
Dawes St	12 C3
De Mere Clo	23 E3
Deacon Clo	4 D6
Dean Rd	4 D6
Deangate Rd	27 A4
Deanwood Clo	22 D3
Deanwood Dri	22 D3
Defiant Clo	20 C5
Defoe Clo	20 C5
Delce Rd	3 D4
Denbigh Av	14 D5
Denton Rd	13 H4
Derby Rd	21 E1
Derwent Way	14 D6
Detling Clo	14 C4
Devon Clo, Rainham	15 F5
Devon Clo, Wayfield	20 C4
Devonshire Rd	12 D2
Dial Rd	13 F2
Dickens Ct	4 B2
Dickens Rd	10 C6
Dickensian Clo	28 A5
Dignals Clo	15 F4
Dillywood La	4 D4
Dixwell Clo	22 D4
Dock Rd	11 F3
Doddington Rd	14 D3
Doggetts Row	27 C2
Doggetts Sq	9 H1
Dogwood Clo	25 G5
Dolphin Dri	23 E4
Dombey Clo, Higham	4 A3
Dombey Clo, Rochester	10 D6
Donet Clo	22 D3
Dongola Rd	5 F5
Dorchester Clo	26 B4
Dornden Gdns	25 E3
Dorritt Way	10 D6
Dorset Sq	14 D5
Dotterel Clo	25 F4
Dove Clo	20 B5
Downside	9 F1
Downsview	20 C3
Drakes Av	5 E5
Drewery Dri	22 C3
Duchess Clo	4 D6
Duchess of Kent Dri	25 E3
Dukes Meadow Dri	21 F6
Duncan Rd	12 D3
Dunkirk Dri	19 F5
Dunnings La	10 D4
Durham Rd	12 C2
Durling Ct	15 H5
Durrell Gdns	20 C2
Duval Dri	19 E3
Dux Court Rd	27 B4
Ealing Clo	25 E2
Earl Clo	25 E2
East Court Green	13 H4
East Hill	20 D3
East Rd	11 G1
East Row	3 C4
East St, Chatham	11 G5
East St, Gillingham	12 D2
Eastcourt La	13 H4
Eastern Rd	13 F2
Eastgate	3 C4
Eastgate Ct	3 C4
Eastgate Ter	3 C4
Eastling Clo	14 D3
Eden Av	19 G4
Eden Rd	27 C3
Edinburgh Rd, Gillingham	12 D3
Edinburgh Rd, Grain	27 C2
Edinburgh Rd, Luton	20 C1
Edisbury Walk	22 D3
Edward St, Chatham	11 H5
Edward St, Frindsbury	5 F6
Edwards Clo	22 C3
Edwin Rd	14 C5
Elaine Av	9 E2
Eldon St	11 G4
Elgin Gdns	8 D3
Elham Clo	13 H5
Elizabeth Ct	14 C5
Ellison Way	15 G4
Elm Av, Chatham	19 F2
Elm Av, Chattenden	6 C3
Elm Clo	4 B2
Elm Rd	13 E2
Elm Tree Dri	9 G6
Elmfield	13 G5
Elmhurst Gdns	11 E5
Elmstone Rd	23 E2
Elmwood Rd	6 B2
Ely Clo	15 E4
Embassy Clo	21 F2
Emerald Clo	18 D4
Emily Rd	20 B5
Englefield Cres	26 B4
Enterprise Clo	11 E1
Epaul La	10 C2
Ernest Rd	11 G6
Esplanade, Rochester	3 A3
Esplanade, Strood	9 H2
Essex Rd	16 C3
Estelle Clo	18 D4
Ethelbert Rd	9 H4
Eton Clo	24 C2
Eva Rd	12 D5
Everest Dri	7 G3
Everest La	5 F5
Everest Mews	7 G3
Evergreen Clo	21 G6
Ewart Rd	19 E2
Exeter Walk	18 D4
Exmouth Rd	12 C1
Exton Clo	25 F4
Fairfax Clo	22 D4
Fairlead Rd	* 18 D2
Fairview Av	21 H6
Fairview Dri	4 A2
Fairway Clo	18 D2
Falkland Pl	24 C5
Fallowfield	19 H3
Fanconi Clo	25 E3
Fane Way	22 D4
Farley Clo	25 G4
Farm Hill Av	5 E5
Farm Rd	24 B3
Farmdale Av	9 F6
Farnham Clo	15 H5
Farraday Clo	19 E3
Featherby Rd	13 G4
Feldspar Clo	24 D5
Fellows Clo	21 H5
Fernbank Clo	24 C4
Ferndale Rd	13 E3
Ferndown Clo	22 B4
Ferrier Clo	23 E4
Ferry Rd	16 D4
Field Clo	19 E5
Fieldworks Rd	11 G1
Finwell Rd	15 G4
Fir Tree Gro	25 G5
Fire Thorne Clo	13 E2
First Av, Gillingham	13 E6
First Av, Luton	20 C1
Fisher Rd	20 B4
Five Elms La	11 E4
Flamingo Clo	20 B5
Flaxmans Ct	12 A2
Fleet Rd	18 D2
Flint Grn	25 F3
Florence St	5 F6
Foord St	10 D4
Fordwich Grn	14 C3
Forest Dale Rd	24 D6
Forest Dri	24 C4
Foresters Clo	24 C4
Forge La, Gillingham	13 E2
Forge La, High Halstow	27 B4
Forge La, Higham	4 A3
Formby Rd	16 C3
Fort Pitt Hill	11 E4
Fort Pitt St	11 E5
Fort St	10 D4
Fostington Way	24 C5
Foulds Clo	22 C4
Fountain Rd	4 D5
Four Elms Hill	6 B4
Fourth Av	13 E4
Fourwents Rd	7 F1
Fowey Clo	20 C6
Fowler Clo	22 C6
Fox Burrow Clo	22 D4
Fox St	12 C2
Foxglove Cres	24 B2
Francis Dri	24 D4
Franklin Rd	12 D3
Franks Ct	14 C4
Frederick Rd	14 C4
Frederick St	11 G5
Freeman Gdns	19 G2
Frensham Walk	24 C4
Freshwater Rd	20 B4
Fresia Clo	13 F3
Friar Av	24 C4
Friary Place	9 H1
Frindsbury Hill	5 G5
Frindsbury Rd	5 F6
Frinsted Clo	14 D3
Frittenden Rd	5 H4
Fry Clo	27 C1
Fulmar Rd	8 D3
Furrells Rd	3 D3
Gads Hill	13 F2
Gainsborough Clo	23 E2
Galahad Av	9 E2
Galbri Dri	9 F2
Galena Clo	24 D5
Garden St	11 G2
Gardenia Clo	5 G4
Gardner St	12 D3
Garfield Rd	12 D2
Gashouse Rd	3 A3
Gatcombe Clo	20 B6
Gayhurst Clo	22 D2
Geneva Av	13 G6
Gentian Clo	24 C2
George La	3 A3
Georgian Way	22 C5
Gerald Av	11 G6
Gerrard Av	19 E3
Gibraltar Av	11 G2
Gibraltar Hill	3 B2
Gilbert Clo	21 G6
Gill Av	5 H3
Gillingham Grn	13 E2
Gillingham Rd	12 D4
Gills Cottages	11 E4
Gills Ct	11 E1
Gladstone Rd	11 E6
Gladwyn Clo	22 D4
Glamford Rd	8 D3
Glamis Clo	20 B6
Glanville Rd, Gillingham	13 E3
Glanville Rd, Strood	5 F6
Gleaming Wood Dri	25 F6
Gleanings Mews	9 H3
Glebe Rd	13 E5
Glencoe Rd	11 E6
Glenwood Clo, Hempstead	21 G4
Glenwood Clo, Upper Luton	20 D2
Glistening Glade	23 E3
Globe La	3 B1
Gloucester Clo	15 G6
Glovers Mill	10 D5
Glynne Clo	23 E3
Goad Av	25 E2
Goddings Dri	9 G5
Goddington Rd	5 F5
Godfrey Clo	5 E4
Golden Wood Clo	25 G5
Goldsmith Rd	12 D4
Goldstone Walk	24 D5
Goodall Clo	23 E3
Goodwin Rd	26 C4
Goodwood Clo	27 C4
Goose Clo	20 B5
Gordon Rd, Brompton	11 G1
Gordon Rd, Chatham	11
Gordon Rd, Gillingham	13
Gordon Rd, Hoo	7
Gordon Rd, Strood	5
Gordon Ter	9
Gorse Av	24
Gorse Rd	5
Gorst St	12
Goudhurst Rd	13
Gould Rd	25
Grafton Av	19
Graham Clo	11
Grain Rd, Grain	27
Grain Rd, Lwr Stoke	28
Grain Rd, Wigmore	22
Granary Clo	15
Grange Hill	11
Grange Rd, Gillingham	13
Grange Rd, Strood	5
Grange Way	22
Grant Clo	9
Granville Rd	13
Grasmere Gro	5
Grassey Glade	21
Gravel Walk	3
Graveney Clo	26
Gravesend Rd	4
Grayne Av	27
Great Lines	11
Great South Av	19
Grebe Clo	28
Green Banks	19
Green Clo	18
Green La, Cliffe	26
Green La, Grain	27
Green St	12
Green Way	19
Greenacre	19
Greenbank Clo	22
Greenfield Rd	13
Greenfields Clo	5
Greenfinches	5
Greenvale Gdns	13
Greenview Walk	13
Greenwich Clo	25
Gregory Clo	23
Grosvenor Av	11
Grosvenor Rd	5
Grove Rd, Gillingham	13
Grove Rd, Luton	20
Grove Rd, Strood	5
Grove Rd, Upr Halling	5
Guardian Ct	14
Guildford Gdns	8
Gun La	3
Gundulph Rd	3
Gundulph Sq	3
Gunnis Clo	22
Hadleigh Ct	11
Haig Av, Chatham	11
Haig Av, Gillingham	13
Haig Av, Rochester	19
Haig Villas	6
Hale Rd	26
Halifax Clo	19
Hall Rd	25
Halling By Pass	16
Hallsfield Rd	24
Hallwood Clo	22
Ham La	25
Hamelin Rd	21
Hamilton Ct	20
Hamilton Rd	3
Hammond Hill	3
Hampshire Clo	20
Hampton Clo	20
Hamwick Grn	25
Hanover Dri	22
Hanway	21
Harcourt Gdns	23
Hardinge Clo	22
Hards Town	11
Hardy Clo	11
Hare St	11
Harebell Clo	24
Haredale Clo	18
Harold Av	11
Harold Rd	16
Harptree Dri	24
Harrison Dri	7
Harrow Rd	3
Hartington St	11
Hartpiece Clo	15
Harty Av	22
Harvel Av	9
Harvesters Clo	24
Harvey Rd	15
Harwood Rd	15
Hatfield Rd	13

Name	Ref
...haway Clo	9 H3
...ton Rd	25 F3
...en Clo	18 D1
...isham Clo	10 D6
...vbeck Rd	22 D5
...vkhurst Rd	13 G5
...vkins Clo	11 G2
...vkwood Clo	10 D4
...vthorn Rd	8 D2
...vthorne Av	14 C4
...vthorns	24 D5
...es Clo	4 B3
...fields	25 G4
...ley Clo	16 B1
...men St	11 E5
...ward Av	5 F6
...el Gro	19 H3
...lemere Dri	13 G3
...dcorn Rd	13 H4
...ther Clo	24 C1
...thfield Clo	20 C4
...npstead Rd	22 A6
...npstead Valley Dri	22 B3
...ley Clo, Rainham	15 E6
...ley Clo, Wayfield	20 B5
...ry St, Chatham	11 H5
...ry St, Rainham	15 G5
...plewhite Mews	24 C5
...bert Rd, Chatham	11 G5
...bert Rd, Rainham	15 E6
...dsdown	7 E2
...eford Clo	15 E4
...tage Clo	20 B5
...tage Dri	21 F2
...man Ter	11 G5
...mitage Rd	4 B2
...ne Rd	14 C4
...o Walk	18 D4
...on Way, Lwr Stoke	28 B4
...on Way, Wayfield	20 C3
...er Croft	9 F3
...ory Dell	22 B3
...ins La	3 B1
...Dewar Rd	15 G6
...Elms	15 E4
...Ridge	21 F2
...St, Brompton	11 G2
...St, Chatham	3 A1
...St, Gillingham	12 C3
...St, Grain	27 C2
...St, Halling	16 C3
...St, Rainham	15 F5
...St, Rochester	3 A3
...St, Strood	5 F6
...St, Upr Upnor	6 B6
...View	4 B2
...am Rd, Cliffe	26 A2
...am Rd, Wainscott	5 H2
...field Rd	22 D1
...field Rd	22 D1
...grove Rd	20 B6
...lands Clo	8 D3
...woods Clo	4 A2
...a Rd	11 G5
...Chase	24 B3
...Ct	6 B3
...Farm Clo	27 C4
...Rd, Rochester	9 G6
...Rd, Wouldham	17 A6
...View Way	19 E6
...orough Gro	24 D3
...rest Dri	16 C2
...rest Rd	11 F6
...Ter	11 F5
...haw Cres	8 D3
...ide	17 B1
...ide Av	5 F5
...ide Rd	11 G5
...op Rd	5 G4
...iew Cotts	27 C4
...field Clo	5 E5
...an Rd	26 C4
...on Cres	21 G5
...th Clo	21 H4
...th La	21 H4
...th Way	14 B6
...orn La	3 B1
...ombe Rd, Chatham	11 F6
...ombe Rd, ...ochester	10 D5
...ler Clo	20 C5
...ling St	15 F5
...and Rd	24 B2
...ngsbourne Rd	14 D3
...y Clo, Gillingham	13 E2
...y Clo, Wayfield	20 C3
...y Rd, Strood	9 E3
Holly Rd, Wainscott	5 H3
Hollytree Dri	4 A2
Hollywood La	5 G3
Holmoaks	15 E4
Holmside	13 E6
Holtwood Clo	22 D3
Homewards Rd	28 A2
Hone St	5 F6
Honey Clo	21 G6
Honeybee Glade	23 E3
Honeypot Clo	5 G5
Honeysuckle Clo	24 C2
Hoo Common	6 C3
Hoo Rd	6 A4
Hook Clo	24 B1
Hoopers Pl	10 D4
Hoopers Rd	10 D4
Hope St	11 G5
Hopewell Dri	20 C3
Hornbeam Av	25 E3
Horrid Hill	14 D1
Horseshoe Clo	21 F6
Horsewash La	3 A3
Horsley Rd	9 H4
Horsted Av	19 F2
Horsted Way	19 E4
Horwood Clo	17 D3
Hospital Hill	21 H5
Hospital La	11 E4
Hothfield Rd	15 F5
Houghton Av	22 B5
Howard Av	10 D5
Howbury Walk	22 D5
Huckleberry Clo	25 E3
Hudson Clo	14 G5
Hughes Dri	11 G5
Humber Cres	9 F1
Hunstanton Clo	23 E5
Hunters Way	21 E2
Hunters Way West	21 E2
Huntersfield Clo	25 F4
Huntsmans Clo	19 E2
Hurst Clo	19 E5
Hurst Hill	24 B4
Hurst Pl	15 F6
Hurstwood	24 B2
Hutsford Clo	22 D3
Hyacinth Rd	8 D2
Hybrid Clo	18 D2
Hyperion Dri	5 E4
Iden Rd	5 G4
Idenwood Clo	22 D3
Illustrious Clo	20 B5
Imperial Rd	12 C5
Impton La	24 D6
INDUSTRIAL ESTATES:	
Arden Bus. Pk	11 E1
Beechings Way Ind Est	13 G4
Elm Court Ind Est	25 H3
Henley Bus. Pk	11 E2
Horsted Retail Pk	18 D5
Neptune Bus. Est	11 E1
Riverside Est	11 E2
Spectrum Bus. Pk	11 E1
Victory Bus. Pk	11 E1
Ingle Rd	11 F6
Ingram Rd	13 E2
Institute Rd	11 G5
Iona Clo	25 G5
Ironside Clo	19 G3
Irvine Rd	4 A3
Ivers Gate Clo	15 F4
Ivy Pl	17 B1
Ivy St	15 F6
Jacklin Clo	24 C3
Jackson Av	19 E3
Jackson Clo	14 D5
James Rd	16 B1
James St, Chatham	3 C2
James St, Rochester	10 D4
Japonica Clo	25 F4
Jarrett Av	5 H3
Jasmin Clo	24 C2
Jasper Av	11 G6
Jefferson Dri	14 D5
Jeffery St	12 D3
Jenkins Dale	11 F5
Jenner Rd	10 D4
Jennifer Ct	7 G3
Jersey Rd	5 E6
Jeyes Rd	12 C4
Jeyes St	11 G5
Jezreels Rd	12 D6
Jiniwin Rd	18 D4
John St	10 D4
Joiners Ct	19 H1
Jubilee Ter	12 C2
Judkins Clo	20 C5
Junction Rd	12 D4
Juniper Clo	24 D2
Jutland Clo	28 C2
Kellaway Rd	24 D4
Kemp Clo	24 B2
Kemps Wharf Rd	15 F2
Kempton Clo	25 F3
Kendal Way	14 D6
Kenilworth Dri	22 D2
Kenilworth Gdns	23 E2
Kennard Clo	9 E6
Kennington Clo	13 H4
Kent Clo	17 D3
Kent Rd	16 C3
Kenwood Av	24 D2
Kenyon Walk	22 C5
Keston Ct	14 A4
Kestrel Rd	25 F4
Keyes Av	11 G6
Khartoum Rd	11 F3
Khyber Rd	11 G1
Killick Rd	7 F2
Kimberley Rd	12 D5
King Arthurs Dri	5 E4
King Edward Rd, Chatham	11 F6
King Edward Rd, Gillingham	13 F2
King Edward Rd, Rochester	9 H3
King George Rd	19 F6
King St, Chatham	3 D1
King St, Gillingham	12 D3
King St, Rochester	3 D4
King William Rd	12 D1
Kingfisher Dri	20 C4
Kings Av	9 H5
Kings Bastion	11 G3
Kings Orchard	3 B4
Kings Rd	20 D2
Kingsdale Ct	20 D2
Kingsdown Clo	22 B4
Kingshill Dri	7 F1
Kingsnorth Rd	14 C2
Kingsnorth Cres	25 E1
Kingsway	21 E2
Kingswood Av	11 F6
Kingswood Rd, Blue Bell Hill	24 A6
Kingswood Rd, Gillingham	12 D2
Kinross Clo	20 B4
Kirby Rd	6 B2
Kirkdale Clo	25 G4
Kit Hill Av	24 B3
Kitchener Av	19 G2
Kitchener Cotts	28 C4
Kitchener Rd, Chattenden	6 B3
Kitchener Rd, Frindsbury	5 F5
Knavesacre Ct	22 D4
Knight Av	13 E2
Knight Rd	9 G2
Knights Clo	7 F2
Knights Rd	7 F2
Knowle Rd	25 F3
Kyetop Walk	23 E3
La Providence	3 B3
Laburnum Rd	8 D3
Ladyclose Av	26 B4
Ladyfields	25 G4
Ladywood Rd	16 B1
Laker Rd	18 C5
Lakewood Dri	22 C3
Lambarde Av	19 E3
Lamberhurst Grn	13 H5
Lambes Ct	22 D3
Lambeth Clo	25 E2
Lambourn Way	25 F3
Lambourne Pl	15 G3
Lambs Frith Grove	22 B5
Lamplighters Clo	21 G6
Lancaster Ct	22 C2
Lancelot Av	4 D6
Lancelot Clo	9 E2
Landor Ct	22 B6
Langdale Clo	14 D5
Langdon Rd	9 H4
Lankester Parker Rd	18 C5
Lansdowne Rd	11 E6
Lapwing Rd	27 C2
Larch Croft	24 D2
Larch Wood Clo	25 G5
Larkfield Rd	13 E4
Larkin Clo	5 G4
Larkspur Rd	24 C2
Laura Pl	17 B1
Laurel Rd	12 C1
Laurel Walk	23 E2
Lavenda Clo	22 B4
Lavender Clo	24 B2
Lawn Clo	19 H1
Lawrence St	12 C3
Layfield Rd	13 F2
Leafy Glade	21 H5
Leander Rd	18 D4
Leander Walk	18 D4
Lee Green Rd	5 G1
Leeds Sq	13 H5
Leet Clo	13 E2
Leeward Rd	18 D2
Leitch Row	11 G2
Lendrim Clo	11 G2
Lenham Way	13 G5
Lennox Row	11 G2
Leonard Rd	12 C6
Leopold Rd	11 G5
Leslie Rd	12 D1
Lester Rd	11 G5
Letchworth Av	19 F2
Levett Clo	27 C1
Lewis Av	11 G6
Leybourne Clo	24 D4
Leybourne Rd	4 D6
Leyton Av	21 E2
Lidsing Rd	22 A6
Lilac Cres	8 D3
Lilac Rd	8 D3
Lillechurch Rd	26 A4
Lime Ct	22 C5
Limetree Clo	19 H3
Lincoln Clo	8 C2
Lincoln Rd	12 D1
Linden Rd	13 E3
Lineacre Clo	22 D3
Lines Ter	3 D1
Lingley Dri	5 G4
Linton Dann Clo	7 F1
Lintorn Simmonds Rd	6 B3
Linwood Av	4 C6
Listmas Rd	11 H5
Little John Av	24 C4
Littlebourne Av	13 H4
Livingstone Circus	13 E3
Livingstone Rd	13 E3
Lobelia Clo	13 E2
Locarno Av	13 G6
Lochat Rd	6 A1
Lock St	3 C4
Lockington Gro	3 C4
Locksley Clo	24 B4
Lodge Hill La	6 B2
Lombardy Clo	22 B3
London Rd, Rainham	14 C5
London Rd, Strood	5 E6
Long Catlis Rd	22 D4
Longfellow Rd	12 D1
Longfield Av	27 C3
Longford Clo	15 G6
Longhill Av	11 H5
Longhurst Dri	24 C4
Longley Rd, Rainham	15 C3
Longley Rd, Rochester	10 D4
Lonsdale Dri	23 E3
Lords Wood Clo	25 E4
Lords Wood La	20 C6
Louisville Av	13 E4
Love La	3 A4
Lovelace Clo	23 E3
Lower Rainham Rd	13 H2
Lower Rochester Rd	5 E2
Lower Twydall La	14 C2
Lower Woodlands Rd	13 F2
Lubbock Walk	23 E4
Lumsden Ter	11 E4
Luton High St	20 D1
Luton Rd	11 H5
Lyall Way	25 F3
Lydd Rd	20 B6
Lyle Clo	5 F5
Lyminge Clo	14 C3
Lyndhurst Av	22 C1
Lynette Av	5 E4
Lynors Av	5 E4
Lynstead Rd	13 H5
Lynton Dri	25 E3
McCudden Row	11 G2
Macdonald Rd	12 D2
McKenzie Rd	24 D3
Macklands Way	15 G3
Madden Av	19 E6
Mafeking Rd	24 C3
Magdalen Clo	22 B5
Magnolia Av	22 C4
Magpie Hall Rd	11 G6
Magpie La	23 G6
Maida Rd	11 H6
Maidstone Rd, Bridgewood	24 A2
Maidstone Rd, Chatham	3 B2
Maidstone Rd, Rainham	15 E6
Maidstone Rd, Rochester	3 C4
Maidstone Rd, Wigmore	22 D4
Main Gate Rd	11 F2
Main Rd	6 C3
Mallard Way	28 B4
Mallingdene Clo	26 C3
Mallow Way	24 C2
Malmaynes Hall Rd	28 A5
Malt Mews	10 C3
Malta Av	19 G4
Malvern Rd	13 E6
Manchester Clo	20 C5
Manor La	9 F6
Manor Rd	3 A2
Manor St	11 G2
Mansell Dri	9 F6
Mansion Row	11 G2
Maple Av	13 E3
Maple Rd	9 E2
Maplins Clo	15 F5
Marathon Paddock	12 D4
Mardale Clo	15 G5
Marden Rd	5 G4
Margate Clo	13 E2
Margetts Pl	6 C4
Marion Clo	24 D3
Maritime Clo	11 E1
Market Pl	3 B3
Marlborough Rd	11 H4
Marley Rd	7 F1
Marley Way	10 D6
Marlowe Copse	24 C5
Marsh Cres	27 C4
Marsh La	26 B1
Marsh Rd	16 D3
Marsh St	5 G6
Marshall Rd	14 C5
Marshland Vw	28 C3
Marston Clo	24 B3
Marston Walk	24 B3
Martin Rd	5 F6
Maryland Ct	23 E4
Masefield Dri	26 B3
Mathews Way	28 C2
Matilda Clo	21 H3
Matts Hill Rd	23 E6
Maunders Clo	20 C3
Maxwell Rd	11 G3
May Rd, Gillingham	12 C4
May Rd, Rochester	10 D5
May St	16 B1
May Ter	11 G1
Mayfair	5 G5
Mayfield Clo	15 E4
Mayford Clo	25 G4
Maynard Pl	13 E6
Maywood Av	24 B2
Mead Green	25 F3
Mead Wall	26 A1
Meadow Bank Rd	11 H4
Meadow Clo, Chatham	19 F6
Meadow Clo, Upr Halling	16 A4
Meadow Clo, Wigmore	22 B4
Meadow Cres	16 A4
Meadside Walk	19 F5
Medlar Gro	22 B4
Medway Av	27 C3
Medway Rd, Gillingham	12 C1
Medway Rd, Rainham	15 F5
Medway St	3 A1
Meeting House La	3 C2
Megby Clo	23 E3
Melbourne Rd	11 G5
Melody Clo	22 C5
Melville Ct	11 G2
Mercury Clo	9 G6
Meresborough La	23 G4
Meresborough Rd	23 G3
Merevale Grn	25 E2
Mereworth Clo	13 G5
Mermaid Clo	20 B5
Merrals Wood Rd	8 D3
Merryboys Rd	26 B3
Merton Clo	25 F1
Micawber Clo	11 G2
Middle St	11 G2
Middlefields	15 G6
Middleton Clo	23 E4
Mierscourt Clo	15 G6
Mierscourt Rd	15 F6
Milburn Rd	12 C1
Miles Pl	10 D5

Military Rd	3 B1	North Rd, Cliffe	26 B1	Peverel Grn	22 D5
Mill Clo	5 F5	North St	5 F6	Pheasant Rd	20 C1
Mill La, Blue Bell Hill	24 A5	North Ter	6 B1	Phillips Ct	13 H6
Mill La, Luton	20 C2	Northbourne Rd	13 H4	Phoenix Rd	25 E4
Mill Rd, Frindsbury	5 F5	Northcote Rd	9 F2	Pickles Way	26 A1
Mill Rd, Gillingham	12 C2	Northumberland Av	15 F5	Pickwick Cres	10 D6
Millcroft Rd	26 B2	Northwood Av	27 C3	Pier Approach Rd	12 D1
Miller Way	5 H4	Norton Gro	24 B2	Pier Pl	6 C5
Millfields	25 G4	Norwich Clo	8 C3	Pier Rd	12 D1
Millfordhope Rd	4 B6	Norwood Clo	26 B2	Pikefields	14 C3
Mills Ter	11 G5	Nottingham Walk	8 D3	Pilgrims Way, Cuxton	16 C1
Milner Rd	12 D1	Nursery Rd	15 E6	Pilgrims Way, Rushdean	9 E4
Milstead Rd	14 C3	Nutfield Clo	20 C3	Pilgrims Way,	
Milton Av	26 B3			Upr Halling	16 A4
Milton Rd	12 D5	Oak Av	13 E2	Pilgrims Way,	
Mincers Clo	25 E4	Oak Dri	4 A2	Wouldham	17 A6
Minerva Rd	5 E6	Oak Rd	9 E2	Pilot Rd	17 D3
Minor Canon Row	3 B4	Oakhurst Clo	24 C2	Pimpernel Way	24 B2
Minster Rd	14 C3	Oakland Clo	24 C2	Pine Gro	21 G5
Miskin Rd	7 F2	Oakleigh Clo	24 B4	Pine Rd	9 F2
Mitchell Av	11 F6	Oaks Dene	24 C5	Pinewood Dri	25 G6
Mitre Rd	9 H4	Oakum Ct	19 H1	Pintail Clo	27 D2
Monarch Clo	20 B5	Oastview	15 G6	Pippin Croft	22 B3
Monkwood Clo	17 D3	Old Barn Clo	21 F5	Pirbright Clo	25 G4
Monmouth Clo	15 E4	Old Castle Walk	23 E5	Plantation Rd	13 G2
Montford Rd, Frindsbury	5 F6	Old Guard House	27 C2	Pleasant Row	11 G2
Montford Rd,		Old Pattens La	11 E6	Plomley Clo	22 D5
Walderslade	24 C3	Old Rd	3 B2	Ploughmans Way	23 E2
Montgomery Av	19 H4	Old School Ct	6 B3	Plover Clo	25 F4
Montgomery Rd	12 C5	Old Watling St	4 A6	Pluckley Clo	14 C3
Montrose Av	21 E1	Oldfield Clo	14 D6	Plumtree Gro	22 B4
Moonstone Dri	25 E3	Oliver Clo	20 C1	Poachers Clo	20 C6
Moor Park Clo	15 G6	Olivine Clo	24 D5	Podkin Wood	24 C5
Moor St	15 H6	Olliffe Clo	24 4C	Polhill Dri	24 C4
Moore St	5 F5	Onslow Rd	10 D5	Poplar Clo	9 F3
Mooring Rd	18 D2	Opal Grn	25 E4	Poplar Rd	9 E3
Morden St	10 C4	Orange Ter	3 D4	Poplicans Rd	16 B1
Morement Rd	7 F1	Orbit Clo	24 D6	Port Clo	25 E3
Morgan Clo	23 E4	Orchard Av	5 E5	Port Victoria Rd	27 D2
Mortimer Av	26 B3	Orchard St	15 E6	Portland Rd	13 E2
Moss Bank	24 D3	Orchard Villas	11 F5	Portland St	11 H6
Mossy Glade	23 E3	Orchid Clo	8 C2	Portsmouth Clo	8 D2
Motney Hill Rd	15 G2	Ordnance St	11 E5	Portway Rd	26 C4
Mount Pleasant	11 H5	Ordnance Ter	3 A2	Post Barn Rd	11 G6
Mount Rd, Borstal	9 G6	Orion Rd	17 D4	Pottery Rd	7 F2
Mount Rd, Chatham	11 F5	Ormsby Grn	23 E5	Povey Av	5 G3
Mountbatten Av, Higham	4 B2	Osborne Rd	12 D3	Powlett Rd	5 G5
Mountbatten Av,		Osprey Av	21 E1	Preston Av	21 E2
Wayfield	19 G4	Otterham Quay La	15 H6	Preston Way	14 C4
Moyle Clo	23 E4	Otway St, Chatham	11 G5	Pretoria Rd, Chatham	11 G6
Mulberry Clo	22 B5	Otway St, Gillingham	12 D2	Pretoria Rd, Gillingham	12 D5
Murray Rd	5 G5	Otway Ter	11 G5	Prices Cotts	26 C3
Myrtle Cres	19 F6	Owens Way	13 G2	Priestfield Rd	13 E3
		Oxford Rd	12 D5	Priestfields	9 G6
Nags Head La	10 D4			Primrose Av	22 C4
Napier Rd	12 D5	Paget St	12 C3	Primrose Clo	19 E4
Napwood Clo	22 D3	Pagitt St	11 E6	Primrose Rd	16 A3
Nares Rd	23 E5	Palace Ct	12 D6	Prince Arthur Rd	12 B2
Nash Clo	25 E4	Palmers Ter	28 C3	Prince Charles Av	25 E2
Nashenden La	17 B1	Palmerston Rd	11 F6	Princes Av	19 H6
Natal Rd	11 G6	Pankhurst Rd	7 E1	Princes St	10 D5
Neale St	11 F6	Pannell Rd	27 C2	Princess Mary Av	11 H1
Nelson Ct	20 D2	Panton Clo	25 E2	Prinys Dri	22 C5
Nelson Rd	12 D4	Papion Gro	24 B4	Priory Ct	13 G6
Nelson Ter	20 D2	Parham Rd	11 F6	Priory Rd, Strood	9 F2
Neptune Clo	11 E1	Park Av	13 E6	Priory Rd, Twydall	13 G6
Neville Rd	11 E6	Park Cres	19 F3	Prospect Av	5 G5
New Covenant Pl	11 E4	Parker Clo	23 E4	Prospect Pl	17 B1
New Cut	3 A2	Parkfield Rd	15 F4	Prospect Row,	
New Rd, Chatham	3 B2	Parkfields	4 B6	Brompton	11 G2
New Rd, Cliffe	26 B2	Parkside	26 B4	Prospect Row, Chatham	11 G5
New Rd Av	3 A2	Parr Av	12 D2	Pudding Rd	15 G6
New Stairs	11 F3	Parsonage La	5 G5	Puffin Rd	27 C2
New Street	11 F5	Pasley Rd	11 G2	Pump La	14 D4
Newark Yd	9 G1	Pasley Rd East	11 H1	Purbeck Rd	11 F6
Newbury Clo	26 B3	Pasley Rd North	11 H1		
Newenden Rd	5 H4	Pasley Rd West	11 H1	Queen St, Chatham	3 D2
Newitt Rd	7 F2	Patrixbourne Av	14 C4	Queen St, Rochester	10 D4
Newnham Clo	14 D4	Pattens Gdns	19 E1	Queendown Av	22 D3
Newnham St	12 B5	Pattens La	19 E1	Queens Rd, Gillingham	12 D4
Newton Clo	25 F4	Pattens Pl	19 E2	Queens Rd, Luton	20 D2
Nicklaus Dri	24 C3	Payne Ct	22 D5	Queensway	28 C1
Nickleby Clo	10 D6	Pear Tree La	21 E3	Quickrells Av	26 B1
Nightingale Clo	23 F2	Pearman Clo	15 G5	Quickthorn Cres	19 F6
Nile Rd	12 C4	Peartree La	4 A3	Quinion Clo	24 D5
Nine Acres Rd	16 B1	Peckham Clo	5 G5	Quinnell St	15 F5
Norah La	4 A2	Peggotty Clo	4 A3	Quixote Cres	5 F4
Nord Farm Cotts	28 C3	Pelican Clo	8 C2		
Nore Clo	21 E2	Pemberton Sq	5 G5	Railway St, Chatham	3 B2
Norfolk Clo, Rainham	14 D4	Pembroke Gdns	23 F4	Railway St, Gillingham	12 D3
Norfolk Clo,		Pembury Way	15 E4	Rainham Rd	12 D6
Walderslade	25 F3	Penfold Clo	20 B4	Raleigh Clo	20 B5
Norman Clo,		Penguin Clo	8 D2	Ramillies Clo	20 B5
Hempstead	21 H6	Pennant Rd	17 D4	Randall Rd	19 F2
Norman Clo, Rushdean	9 E4	Penshurst Clo	15 E4	Randolph Cotts	5 G5
Norreys Rd	23 E1	Pepys Way	5 E6	Randolph Rd	12 D3
North Bank Clo	9 F3	Perie Row	11 G2	Ranscombe Clo	8 D3
North Dane Way	20 C6	Perry St	11 E5	Ratcliffe Highway,	
North Gate	3 B3	Peterborough Gdns	8 C3	Allhallows	28 A2
North Rd, Brompton	11 G1	Petham Grn	14 C3	Ratcliffe Highway,	
Chattenden	6 C3	St Georges Walk	
Ravenswood Av	5 G5	St James Clo	
Readscroft Rd	22 D4	St James Rd	
Rectory Grange	18 C1	St Johns Clo	
Redbridge Clo	25 E1	St Johns Rd, Gillingham	
Rede Court Rd	4 C6	St Johns Rd, Higham	
Redfern Av	13 E3	St Johns Rd, Hoo	
Redvers Rd	11 G6	St Johns Way	
Redwing Rd	20 B5	St Leonards Av	
Redwood Clo	25 E4	St Lukes Way	
Reed St	26 B1	St Margarets Banks	
Reedham Cres	26 C4	St Margarets Ct	
Reform Rd	11 H6	St Margarets Dri	
Regency Clo	22 C6	St Margarets Mews	
Regent Rd	12 C4	St Margarets St	
Reginald Av	16 B1	St Marys Gdns	
Renown Rd	25 F4	St Marys Rd, Gillingham	
Repton Way	24 C2	St Marys Rd, Strood	
Resolution Clo	20 B5	St Matthews Dri	
Revenge Rd	25 F5	St Matthews Way	
Rhode St	3 C2	St Michaels Clo	
Richard St, Chatham	3 C2	St Nicholas Gdns	
Richard St, Rochester	10 D5	St Pauls Clo	
Richmond Clo,		St Peter St	
Lords Wood	25 E2	St Werburgh Cres	
Richmond Clo,		St Williams Way	
Upper Upnor	6 B6	Salisbury Av	
Richmond Rd	12 D2	Salisbury Rd,	
Ridge Way	12 C2	Blue Bell Hill	
Ridley Rd	9 H4	Salisbury Rd, Chatham	
Ringwood Clo	15 E6	Sally Port Gdns	
Ripon Clo	14 D3	Salt La	
River Dri	9 E1	Sanctuary Rd	
River St	11 G2	Sandgate Ct	
Roach St	9 G2	Sandhurst Clo	
Roberts Rd	15 E5	Sandown Dri	
Robin Hood La	24 A5	Sandpiper Rd	
Robson Dri	7 F2	Sandringham Rd	
Rochester Av	10 D4	Sandy Dell	
Rochester Bri	9 H2	Sandycroft Rd	
Rochester Cres	7 F1	Saracen Clo	
Rochester Rd, Borstal	17 D5	Sarsen Heights	
Rochester Rd, Cuxton	16 B2	Saunders St, Chatham	
Rochester St	11 F5	Saunders St,	
Rock Av	12 C4	Gillingham	
Roebuck Rd	9 H4	Savage Rd	
Roffen Rd	10 D6	Sawyers Ct	
Rolvenden Av	14 D3	Saxon Clo	
Rolvenden Rd	5 G4	Saxon Way	
Roman Way	9 E4	Saxton St	
Romany Rd	13 H6	Scarlett Clo	
Rome Ter	3 C2	School Av	
Romney Rd	20 B6	School La	
Romsey Clo	4 C5	Scimitar Clo	
Rookery Cres	26 B1	Scotby Av	
Roosevelt Av	19 F4	Scott Av	
Rope Walk	3 C1	Scotteswood Av	
Ropemakers Ct	19 H2	Scotts Ter	
Roper Clo	22 D5	Seagull Rd	
Ropers La	7 H1	Seaton Rd	
Rose St	10 D5	Seaview	
Rosebery Av	19 E1	Seaview Rd	
Rosebery Rd	12 D1	Second Av, Gillingham	
Rosemary Clo	24 C1	Second Av, Luton	
Ross St	10 D4	Secretan Rd	
Rothervale	25 F2	Sedge Cres	
Rover Rd	25 E4	Sedley Clo, Cliffe Woods	
Rowbrocke Clo	22 D5	Sedley Clo, Wigmore	
Rowland Av	21 E2	Selbourne Rd	
Rowland Clo	21 E2	Selinge Grn	
Royal Sovereign Av	11 H1	Selsted Clo	
Roystons Clo	15 F4	Setford Rd	
Rucking Way	14 C3	Settington Av	
Rudge Clo	25 G4	Severn Rd	
Rugby Clo	24 C2	Seymour Rd	
Rush Clo	24 D3	Shackleton Clo	
Rushdean Rd	8 D3	Shakespeare Rd	
Russell Av	15 G6	Shamley Rd	
Russell Ct	11 H5	Shanklin Clo	
Russett Clo	4 D5	Sharfleet Dri	
Rutland Pl	22 D5	Sharon Cres	
Rycaut Clo	22 D5	Sharsted Way	
Ryde Clo	20 C3	Shaw Clo	
Rye St	26 D1	Shaws Way	
Ryegrass Clo	20 C5	Shawstead Rd	
		Shelden Dri	
Sadlers Clo	24 B4	Shelldrake Clo	
Saffron Way	24 C1	Shepherds Gate	
Sailmakers Ct	11 H6	Shepherds Way	
St Alban Walk	11 E5	Shepperton Clo	
St Albans Clo	13 E1	Sheraton Ct	
St Albans Rd	8 C3	Sheridan Clo	
St Andrews Rd	12 D1	Sheriff Dri	
St Andrews Walk	28 C2	Sherman Clo	
St Barnabas Clo	12 D5	Sherwood Av	
St Bartholomews La	11 E4	Ship La	
St Bartholomews Ter	11 E4	Shipwrights Av	
St Davids Rd	28 C2	Shirley Av	
St Edmunds Way	15 H5	Sholden Rd	
St Georges Rd	12 C2	Short La	